FAMILIES IN HISTORY

The Shaws

The Shaws

The Family of George Bernard Shaw

Nathaniel Harris

ILLUSTRATED BY ANDREW FARMER

J M DENT & SONS LTD

First published 1977

Text, © Nathaniel Harris, 1977
Illustrations, © J. M. Dent & Sons Ltd, 1977

Printed and bound in Great Britain by
Morrison & Gibb Ltd, London and Edinburgh
for J. M. Dent & Sons Ltd
Aldine House . Albemarle Street . London

This book is set in 11 on 12 pt Baskerville

ISBN 0 460 06735 4

Contents

Wedding Day

On 17th June 1852, George Carr Shaw married Lucinda Elizabeth Gurly at St Peter's Church in Aungier Street, Dublin.

If the Shaws — a remarkably unsentimental family — kept any pictures or mementos of the occasion, they have not survived the passage of time. But the wedding must have been an eminently respectable one, for bride and groom were gentlefolk, St Peter's was a fashionable church, and the officiating clergyman was the up-and-coming rector of nearby St Bride's, presumably brought in because he was George Carr Shaw's brother-in-law.

No doubt the bride and groom were clad as mid-century convention dictated. Bridal dress had already assumed something like its modern form, with silk or satin, plus lace trimmings and orange blossom. But the groom's outfit preserved the colourful character of early Victorian styles, which had elsewhere already given way to more sombre tones. The coat was light blue, tailed and velvet-collared; under it gleamed a white satin embroidered waistcoat; and the nether parts were covered by close-fitting black pantaloons which tied round the ankles. It is not known whether the bride showed to advantage on the day, but the groom — a rather small man of thirty-eight, with pronouncedly crossed eyes — seems unlikely to have impressed.

Afterwards, as the carriage drew away from St Peter's, Mr Shaw made a move to embrace his wife, and was firmly repulsed. Mrs Shaw herself told the story more than once in later years, with undiminished indignation at her husband's forwardness.

Antecedents

The stories of many British families are enlivened by the adventures of their younger sons. Thanks to the system of primogeniture, by which family estates passed to the oldest male child, younger sons of the gentry often had to make their own way, with the help of such family influence as they could muster. It was the necessities of younger sons that first drew some of the Shaws of Kilkenny to live and work in Dublin, though earlier Shaws must certainly have spent the season in the capital during its eighteenth-century heyday. The Dublin Shaws became a numerous and on the whole successful clan, mainly engaged in business and the professions. Their chief was Sir Robert Shaw, who founded Shaw's (later the Royal) Bank and was made a baronet in 1821. To consolidate his position he acquired Bushy Park, an estate of about fifty acres at Rathfarnham, a few miles outside Dublin, and built himself a fine house there.

Sir Robert's first cousin, Bernard Shaw, remained for some time in the ancestral home, marrying a clergyman's daughter, Frances Carr, and achieving local distinction in the militia and as High Sheriff of Kilkenny. He also entered a law partnership in Dublin, perhaps impressed by the financial successes of his relatives; but he evidently saw himself as an investor rather than an active partner. At any rate he left Kilkenny not for Dublin but for the country round the little village of Oughterard in Galway, where the landscape was less tame and he could hunt and shoot and fish to his heart's content. He is said to have been a superb rider and a crack shot, and might have been happy as an American pioneer. Or he could have been a successful craftsman, for he was a skilful carpenter whose 'study' was in fact a workshop; he even built the boat in which he went on fishing expeditions. But, being a gentleman, Bernard Shaw could never do more than play at such occupations; his role was to run (or neglect) estates, or to engage in (or neglect) a business or profession. As his grandson was to point out a century later, a class system puts many square pegs in round holes.

Bernard Shaw left his Kilkenny estates in the hands of an agent, gradually mortgaging them until there was hardly a penny to spare. His business involvements were even more disastrous: his partner suddenly vanished with a very large sum of Shaw's money. Then Shaw himself died — perhaps from embarrassment — and in 1826 Frances Shaw found herself a poor widow with no less than eleven children to look after.

Here a curious element of romance comes into the story. The clan chief, Sir Robert Shaw, allowed the widow to live rent-free in a cottage he owned in Terenure, the area of Dublin closest to his house at Bushy Park. But the widowed baronet's interest went further than Shavian solidarity: he regularly proposed to Mrs Shaw and was as regularly turned down. It is hard to say which is the more remarkable — the fact that Sir Robert could fall in love (and remain in love) with a woman who had borne fifteen children (four had died in childhood), or the fact that the child-festooned Mrs Shaw was prepared to risk turning down her wealthy benefactor.

Somehow or other Frances Shaw managed to bring up her large family. Four of the five girls were successful in finding husbands (one was the Reverend William George Carroll, who was to officiate at the wedding of George Carr Shaw and Lucinda Elizabeth Gurly), and the oldest is said to have remained a virgin only because she thought herself too good for all her suitors. The boys were less fortunate because their requirements were greater. Only the oldest, Barney (William Bernard), received a university education at Trinity College, Dublin. He was then ordained as a clergyman, which was a 'safe' career; but his prospects of advancement were blighted by his growing eccentricity. Over the years he developed a series of manias, switching abruptly from drink to music, and from religion to voyeurism. Finally, in an asylum, he succeeded in killing himself by shutting his head in a carpet bag. The most successful of the brothers was Richard Frederick, who became a civil servant and eventually chief of staff in the Irish Valuation Office. The rest had to get by as best they could. Two emigrated to Australia; one went blind; and one was George Carr Shaw.

The emigrant brothers had a chance to break free from the trap of gentility; for George Carr Shaw in Dublin there was no escape. If you were poor but genteel, almost every avenue was closed to you. You could not become a workman, or even serve in a shop, without a humiliating loss of caste. Without money you could not study medicine at a university or become articled to a solicitor, let alone set up in business. There was nothing for it but to take a job as a clerk — in a warehouse or factory, of course, not in anything so vulgar as a shop or works dealing directly with the public. And, naturally, shrewd employers took advantage of the situation by making the gentleman-clerk accept a smaller salary in return for accepting his pretensions.

In this fashion George Carr Shaw pottered on for some years. Given his quietly amiable temperament, he may have been happy enough, though he had no significant prospects of advancement. His salary was probably sufficient to sustain his gentility or support a wife and family, but not both; so Shaw chose gentility. Then he had a stroke of luck. In 1845, through some unknown connection — no doubt one of the more influential Shaws — he secured a clerkship in Dublin's Four Courts. The job was a sinecure, one of those left-over offices that carry on being filled for years though their function has disappeared with some change in law or custom. There were many such in the rapidly changing society of the nineteenth century, though the Victorian spirit of reform was already on the offensive against them. Sure enough, the reformers swooped on George Carr Shaw's clerkship, and in 1850 succeeded in having it abolished. This, however, proved another stroke of luck. The eighteenth-century tradition had been that the holder of any governmental or administrative job was a kind of government dependant, 'one of the family', with a right to his share in the 'family' property; and it remained strong enough in the nineteenth century to ensure that agreeable office-holders were not turned off without compensation. For this class, at least, the principle of redundancy payments was recognized.

Shaw received a pension of forty-four pounds a year, which was a substantial sum for a man who was still capable of earning a living on his own account; it was as much as most ordinary working men could hope to earn in their prime.

In effect, Shaw had come into money. Over the following year he took a series of temporary jobs, presumably while he decided on a

10

course of action. Meanwhile, he escorted, courted, and married Lucinda Gurly.

Lucinda's father, Walter Bagnall Gurly, was another feckless, reckless gentleman, mortgaging his small property in County Carlow and lavishly distributing IOUs. And like many others before him, he escaped the worst consequences by marrying a fortune: in 1829 he wed Lucinda Whitcroft, the daughter of a wealthy gentleman with properties in Rathfarnham and County Kilkenny. (This Lucinda is not George Carr Shaw's strong-minded bride, but her mother-to-be.)

Without realizing it, ne'er-do-wells like Walter Gurly performed a significant social function. If such a man wanted a wealthy bride, he was most likely to be welcome in a family that was not quite socially acceptable. He effectively traded his name and gentility for the cash he needed. Both sides benefited, and children born of the union would be both rich and well born. It is by such means that ruling groups are held together: instead of separating into mutually hostile castes, birth and wealth could be brought into alliance even in the rather old-fashioned society of Ireland. A grosser international form of the same phenomenon appeared later in the century, when American heiresses invaded European society by marrying needy aristocrats.

The Whitcrofts were outwardly respectable enough, but the skeletons in their cupboard rattled loudly. John Whitcroft, the father of Gurly's bride, was a mystery man whose origins were obscure: if he knew who his father was, he told nobody; and it is possible that he was illegitimate and/or had been abandoned as a baby. However, he imposed himself successfully on Irish society, and passed as a gentleman of leisure. Yet the source of his wealth can hardly have remained a secret. For John Whitcroft owned a chain of pawnshops in the Dublin slums; and although he often operated through 'front men', at least one large establishment, in Winetavern Street, traded openly under the Whitcroft name. Even in money-minded London, pawnbroking was a thoroughly low occupation; so it can only be assumed that Whitcroft's social acceptance was an example of the hypocritical conspiracy of silence — bought and paid for.

But such situations are never very comfortable, and Lucinda Whitcroft's marriage must have given satisfaction — despite the fact that, years later, Lucinda's brother John was still buying back IOUs given by the generous-minded bridegroom. There were two children of the marriage: Walter John Gurly, who took a medical degree at Trinity College, Dublin, and Lucinda Elizabeth Gurly, who married George Carr Shaw.

Lucinda Elizabeth's mother died when she was nine. Squire Walter was unable or unwilling to keep the little girl at home, so she was sent to live with her Aunt Ellen Whitcroft in Palmerston Place, Dublin. This Ellen was another of the pawnbroker's daughters, and bitterly ashamed of the fact. She was also a hunchback and a spinster, and soon became determined that Lucinda Elizabeth should wipe out the past and compensate for her own misfortunes by making a brilliant marriage.

Lucinda Elizabeth — or Bessie, as she came to be called in the family — lived with her aunt from 1839 until her marriage in 1852 — from her tenth to her twenty-third year. Bessie was trained to be — indisputably — a lady. Or, as she later remarked bitterly, she was educated within an inch of her life. It is hard to guess what made her upbringing quite so onerous. Drill in deportment must have been irksome, but eventually the straight back and majestic carriage became second nature to her; and to do Aunt Ellen justice, she turned her niece into the sort of woman who could dress in rags and still be identified at a glance as a lady. Etiquette was more formal and elaborate than it is now, extending from the correct use of finger-bowls to the proper timing of a visit; but the rules were not impossibly difficult and, besides, had to be learned by every gentle-woman. As a compensation, the academic load was light. Bessie employed her own language ably enough, but her only foreign language, French, was for display rather than use; her mastery of it was apparently confined to two fables by La Fontaine, which she could recite with an absolutely correct French accent. This accomplishment was taught — along with water-colours and music — as one of those graceful, husband-catching skills that most nineteenth-century ladies dropped just as soon as they were safely married. If Bessie ever tried her hand at painting, she kept the fact well hidden in later years (though in old age she was to produce a large number of 'spirit drawings' under the influence of other-worldly beings). But she *was* musical. She sang splendidly and was taught to play the piano — which, ironically, was the only physical torture inflicted on her

12

youth. Her teacher was Johann Bernhard Logier, a German musician who had settled in Dublin and achieved some eminence. Unfortunately, Logier had invented a teaching machine called a chiroplast, which clamped the arms, wrists and hands of the learner into the correct position; he or she could not go wrong since no freedom of movement was permitted. Bessie learned to play, and acquired a thorough proficiency in the technical side of music; but, not surprisingly, she never acquired much feeling for the piano. There must have been a whole generation like her, spoiled by the over-inventive Logier.

It was probably not the deportment or the etiquette or the teaching that made Bessie's youth such a bitter memory. More likely it was the general constraint imposed by living alone, in ladylike fashion, with an old woman. Victorian children did run about and play, though little girls were expected to behave with a decorum that now seems unnatural; but it looks as though Bessie, shut up with Aunt Ellen, was expected to behave like a grown-up lady all the time. Such an existence must have been dull for even a grown-up girl, if her temperament was an active one. In fact the young unmarried woman's life — the tedious round of decorum, dilettantism and needlework — might have been specially designed to make her rush into marriage as promising some kind of fulfilment.

Lucinda Elizabeth Gurly did not exactly rush. She waited until she was twenty-two, enduring home life and presumably enjoying the balls and parties that enlivened the Dublin season and provided ample opportunities for meeting young men. But when Bessie did take the plunge, the event had a curiously improvised air.

The improvisation may have been provoked by a sudden, undignified family rumpus which started when Walter Bagnall Gurly decided to get married again. Bessie's mother had been dead for thirteen years, so his intentions hardly seem impious, but all the same Walter was afraid that the Whitcrofts might disapprove. And that would be awkward, since Walter's brother-in-law, the younger John Whitcroft, held a fistful of the erratic widower's IOUs. Walter's solution, very much in character, was to get married without telling the Whitcrofts. The wedding day was fixed, the arrangements were made . . . But Bessie, who was in on the secret, let it slip while talking to one of her relatives. On the wedding morning, when Walter Gurly left his house to buy some gloves, he found himself accosted and taken into custody for debt.

The storm was short-lived for Walter. He soon talked round his brother-in-law, though we can be sure he didn't pay up. But Bessie was left in an awkward position. Her father believed she had wantonly betrayed him, and raged against her, while her Whitcroft relatives no doubt made her feel inferior as the daughter of such a cad. If life at Palmerston Place had been dull before, it now became distinctly uncomfortable. Bessie decided to break out, and before the dust had settled she announced her imminent marriage to George Carr Shaw.

Why did she choose a mild, cross-eyed, thirty-eight-year-old, with no evident attractions? There is certainly no evidence that she was ever in love with him. It may simply have been that nobody else asked her; for Bessie was the sort of determined young woman who often frightens young men off. But it may equally have been that Bessie, who had spent years under Aunt Ellen's tyrannical régime, deliberately picked a mate who would not be able to dominate her.

Ellen Whitcroft was furious. The match meant the ruin of all her vicarious ambitions; and it also made her feel a fool, incapable of noticing what was happening beneath her nose. For on occasion Ellen had actually encouraged Shaw to act as Bessie's escort, just because he was so obviously harmless. Now she threatened to cut Bessie out of her will if the marriage took place. And when Bessie showed no sign of weakening, Ellen told her flatly that her fiancé was a drunkard.

This at least produced à reaction. Bessie flew to Shaw's lodgings in Lennox Street and put him to the question. To her relief he assured her that he was a teetotaller. Evidently the charge of drunkenness was no more than Aunt Ellen's desperate last attempt to change her niece's mind. Ill-feeling now became so strong between aunt and niece that Bessie moved out before her marriage. But Aunt Ellen did send her a wedding present: a bundle of Walter Gurly's IOUs.

Just before the ceremony, Bessie put her finances in order. She had a little money of her own and she intended not to be deprived of it by an extravagant or defaulting spouse. In those days the husband was still master of the family in law, if not always in fact. He could dispose of any property belonging to his wife — who had no redress

14

Wedding of Bessie and George Carr Shaw

even if he spent the proceeds on another woman. The Married Women's Property Acts were still far in the future; but there were ways in which a well-advised woman could protect herself. Bessie's was to sign a deed transferring her property — Government 3¼ per cent stock, lodged in the Bank of Ireland, to the value of £1,256 — to trustees. With these businesslike preliminaries completed, true love — or whatever it was — could take its course.

And the wedding did take place, only three weeks after that of Walter Gurly, who had calmed down sufficiently to give his only daughter away. And Aunt Ellen Whitcroft did disinherit Bessie — which must have saddened George Carr Shaw, whose prospects would have been much improved by such a substantial windfall. (When the old lady died in 1862, she left almost four thousand pounds.)

Undaunted, the happy pair went off on their honeymoon — which, for reasons likely to remain forever obscure, was spent in a Liverpool hotel.

As Bessie later told the story, she was alone in the hotel and happened to open a wardrobe door. Instead of suits and shirts there were quantities of empty bottles . . . .

Bessie fled from the hotel and made for the docks, with some confused idea of signing on as a stewardess on a ship. But a few remarks from coarse passers-by discouraged and frightened her. Being able to think of nothing better to do, she returned to the hotel — resigned, but bitter in the conviction that Aunt Ellen had been right after all.

The Irish Background

All these dramas of private life were played out by men and women who belonged to a small but powerful minority of the Irish people. As gentlefolk they were in a class minority; as Protestants they were in a religious minority. They have even been classed as a kind of national minority, for in recent years people like the Shaws have been labelled 'Anglo-Irish', rather unfairly identifying them with English rule in Ireland. They never thought of themselves as anything but Irish, and if they spoke only English so did the great majority of the population. Still, like others of their sort they were English by distant descent (Mr Shaw, for example, could trace his ancestry to a seventeenth-century Hampshire gentleman-soldier who came over to Ireland with William III); and in a country where old, unhappy conflicts were remembered for centuries, such facts mattered. If we are to properly understand the Shaws and their city, there is no avoiding a look into Ireland's past.

The English presence in Ireland goes back to the twelfth century, but her modern history begins in the early seventeenth, when Queen Elizabeth's army effectively subdued the country and imposed English Protestant rule on a people who were overwhelmingly Catholic. Half a century later, Oliver Cromwell crushed the rebellious Irish and put the besieged populations of Wexford and Drogheda to the sword. Ireland has never forgiven him for it; but the settlement that followed had far more long-lasting consequences. Over most of the country the Catholic property-owners were evicted, and from that time the ruling class was English in origin and Protestant in religion. They were by no means subservient to English interest or even pro-English; some of the chief defenders of Irish rights were Anglo-Irishmen such as Dean Swift and Grattan, and the first leader of the Irish Nationalists in Parliament was the Protestant gentleman Charles Stuart Parnell. All the same, it must be admitted that the Anglo-Irish

17

were a distinctive, isolated group, thinly spread over Ireland, and therefore potentially vulnerable.

An area to which these remarks do not apply is Ulster, in the north-east. There, in the course of the seventeenth century, large numbers of Scottish and English settlers had been 'planted' in order to tame what was then the wildest of all Irish provinces. The majority of the population was Protestant and drawn from all classes — an exceptional situation that is at the root of the 'Ulster problem' still going strong in the 1960s and 1970s. However, Ulster and her troubles are outside the scope of this book.

The system of class reinforced by religion helped to make Irish society more rigid than its English equivalent. In England a man with money could generally secure acceptance in good society; and at worst his son could do so after a training alongside the sons of gentlemen at one of the newly vigorous public schools. In Ireland birth still counted and, as we have seen, the distinctions between wholesale and retail, merchant and shopkeeper, existed as part of the moral law in Mr Shaw's mind. No doubt the barriers would have come down quickly enough had Ireland experienced an industrial and commercial revolution like England's: when rich men appear in force they either impose themselves on society or overthrow it. But nothing of the sort could happen in Ireland, which was essentially a country of poor peasants, without coal or the other resources needed for industry, and further hampered by English competition. By the eighteen-fifties the Irish linen industry had become concentrated in the north-east, which was also an important shipbuilding centre. The rest of Ireland was an overwhelmingly rural land in which the people subsisted largely on potatoes though exporting a variety of other farm produce. It was only now recovering from the disasters of the previous decade, when successive failures of the potato crop had caused a terrible famine in which a million Irish died and another million were driven to emigrate. The pattern set by the Famine — one of declining population linked with late marriage and continuing emigration — lasted until the mid-twentieth century.

Dublin was less drastically affected, and in fact steadily expanded. But of course the city was held back by the general failure to develop, and could not match the growth of London, Manchester, Birmingham, Glasgow and other British towns. Dublin remained a

Four Courts, Dublin

primarily commercial city from which farm produce, textiles and Guinness were exported, and through which poured manufactured goods from England; but there were a few light industries, and the rivers flowing into Dublin Bay supported paper, flour, corn, silk and textile mills.

The majority of Dublin's three hundred thousand people were Catholics, but the main features of the city were Protestant in origin — either great public buildings created by and for the Crown-appointed administration, presided over by the Viceroy from Dublin Castle, or streets and squares laid out by great aristocratic land-owners. The clubs and banks of Dublin were Protestant institutions, as was the city's pride — the great Guinness brewery at St James's Gate, unmatched in Europe. Even the Protestant churches were grander and more numerous than the Catholic 'chapels'. Since much of the building had been done in the eighteenth century, when good taste was widely diffused and town planning was taken seriously, Dublin was an outwardly impressive city. Public buildings such as Leinster House, the Four Courts (where George Carr Shaw had worked as a clerk), the Custom House beside the River Liffey, the Kings Inns, Trinity College and the Bank of Ireland (formerly the Parliament House) are splendid examples of the eighteenth-century neo-classical style, with their columns, pediments and domes. Wide Street Commissioners were active from 1757, and it is to them that Dublin owes the 150-foot (45m) breadth of what is now called O'Connell Street. Before Republican times it was Sackville Street, Dublin's chief thoroughfare and the main axis of the modern city, to the east of the decaying old town. From Sackville Street you could pass over the Liffey to the south side by the Carlyle Bridge, built in 1792. This took you along Grafton Street to Trinity College, from which it was a few minutes' walk to two of Dublin's finest squares: St Stephen's Green directly south of the College and Merrion Square to the south-east, both comprising rows of unassertively elegant houses with long balconied windows and fine doorways framed with columns and crowned with ornamented semicircular fanlights. Even the canals and ring roads and riverside quays of Dublin were built in the eighteenth century.

But if Dublin was — and is — an admirable eighteenth-century city, it was just because there was no Irish Industrial Revolution to trans-

Poor quarters of Dublin

form it. Dublin missed the benefits of England's progress, but also escaped the worst excesses of Victorian building, which too often entailed the tearing down of the old and beautiful and its replacement by something shoddy, or ugly, or both.

But there was no escaping squalor and decay, though they might sometimes be hidden behind the deceptively impressive façade of an old house. The western part of Dublin, and especially the old city, south of the river, and the 'Liberties' just outside it, was a dense agglomeration of narrow, tortuous streets consisting of overcrowded and typhus-ridden houses. The facts of nineteenth-century urban poverty are well known; here it is enough to quote Karl Marx's friend and collaborator Friedrich Engels, whose *Condition of the Working Classes in 1844* says that in Dublin's poor quarters 'the filth, the uninhabitableness of the houses and the neglect of the streets surpass all description'. It is worth bearing that in mind, for purposes of comparison, when we look into the Shaws' financial condition.

Synge Street

Like other couples, the Shaws came back from their honeymoon and settled down. Mr Shaw was understandably reluctant to become a clerk again, and had probably led Bessie Shaw to expect something better than that. So he took the plunge and sold his pension for a flat £500; the buyer, a Mr O'Brien, thus acquired an income of £44 a year for the duration of Shaw's life — which O'Brien shrewdly insured for £600. In the event he got the best of the bargain, for George Carr Shaw was to live for another thirty-odd years.

Shaw used the lump sum to go into partnership with one George Clibborn; the record is obscure, but it seems likely that he bought into an already existing firm, Clibborn & Moncrief, which now became Clibborn & Shaw, corn and flour merchants. This was wholesale business which involved dealing with other merchants, and with bakers and other retailers; nothing was sold direct to the public, so there was no danger of Clibborn and Shaw compromising their respectability. The firm had an office and warehouse at 67 Jervis Street, a few turnings from the Four Courts. And there was also a flour mill out in the country at Dolphin's Barn, a suburb some two kilometres from the Shaws' new house at No. 3 Synge Street.

Synge Street was not in the suburbs but on the very outskirts of Dublin proper — on the south side of the river, just on the town side of the Grand Canal. It was a side street running off Harrington Street — hardly fashionable, but decent enough and only five minutes' walk from St Stephen's Green to the north. In the eighteen-fifties the street had an unfinished look, for there were only eleven almost new (if rather undistinguished) houses in two terraces, four on one side of the street and seven on the other; the builder's yard stood ready nearby, but for some years no more houses were put up — an indication of the slowness with which Dublin was growing. (Eventually, in the 'sixties, Synge Street was extended over two more streets and the

No 3 Synge Street

Shaws' house was given a new number and name, 33 Upper Synge Street.)

No. 3 was a two-storey, yellow-brick structure with a basement for the servants' quarters, the kitchen and the pantry. The parlour — the most formal room in the house, where guests would be entertained — faced on to the street on the ground floor; behind it stood the nursery and a small spare room which Mr Shaw used as a dressing room. Above the parlour, the drawing room was the informal gathering-place of the family; the other top-floor room was Mr and Mrs Shaw's bedroom. Outside in the little garden patch, at an even greater distance from the family than the servants' quarters, stood a shed containing the w.c.

The house was soon inhabited by as many Shaws as it could hold. Lucinda Frances — 'Lucy' — was born on 26th March 1853, and must therefore have been conceived on the honeymoon. Elinor Agnes — 'Yuppy' — arrived about two years later. And in the person of George Bernard Shaw — 'Bob', born on 26th July 1856 — the family was presented with a male heir. There were no more children, though whether Mrs Shaw thought that three were enough, or simply because there was a shortage of money and space, is not known.

The space problem was solved, when George Bernard grew too big, by moving him into the spare room next to the nursery, which the two girls were left to share. But the money problem seemed insoluble. Mr Shaw seems to have made about three hundred pounds a year from his corn merchant's business, which was simply not enough to keep him and his wife without skimping and worrying. Fluctuations in the economic situation must have made some years still more difficult, and on at least one occasion a defaulting customer almost brought down Clibborn & Shaw; Clibborn burst into tears when he heard the news, and Shaw retired to a corner of the warehouse and laughed until he was exhausted (presumably a hysterical reaction, though it must be admitted that Mr Shaw did possess an overdeveloped sense of anticlimax).

Bankruptcy aside, the Shaws were in no danger of sinking into the ranks of the Dublin poor. Their worries were of a different order, stemming from the disparity between Mr Shaw's income and the standard of living appropriate to his status. It was expensive to be a gentleman with a growing family, and some years it was evidently a struggle to keep up appearances. *The Englishwoman's Domestic Magazine* of 1859 gives us an insight into the situation. One of its articles is entitled 'Can one live on £300 a year?' Given the readership of the magazine, 'live' of course meant 'get married'. The answer, inevitably, was Yes: women's magazines do not thrive by advocating celibate spinsterhood. But it was a qualified Yes. On £300 a year it would be 'frugal marriage', which precluded the husband from laying down a wine cellar or a library, made the wife emphatically a *house*wife, and found its highest joys in domestic companionship and devotion to children. The ideal put forward is one that we think of as typically mid-Victorian, at once strenuous, practical and high-minded.

Mr Shaw seems to have had no markedly extravagant habits, though he would probably have found the tone of *The Englishwoman's Domestic Magazine* rather lower middle class; his notion of gentility was a less moral and more caste-conscious one. The pleasures of domestic endeavour held still less attraction for Mrs Shaw, who had neither the training nor the inclination for housekeeping. She insisted that she must have a maid, a cook and a nurse for the children; later on she would need a governess for them, though she agreed to economize by employing a needy gentlewoman, Miss Caroline Hill, who would accept payment by the hour and not live in.

Actually the servants were not a major expense. They were paid about eight pounds a year — perhaps a pound or two more for the cook, if she was any good; but Mrs Shaw's standards seem not to have been high. The very low price of labour is one of the facts about nineteenth-century society that it is hardest for us to come to terms with, since our own society is one in which (for example) it is often more expensive to have something repaired than to throw it away and buy a new one. In Victorian times, despite the growth of mass-production, it was objects that were generally hoarded and cherished; labour was used up lavishly. Female labour was cheapest of all, since there was no respectable alternative to domestic service: other jobs simply did not exist until the advent of the shorthand-typist in the eighteen-eighties. And, incidentally, the low price of labour accounts for the sexual availability of the working class in this period: a present of a few shillings — little enough to most gentlemen — repre-

26

sented a week's wages or more to a servant girl on her afternoon out. Eight pounds a year moved in a different world from 'Can one live on £300 a year?'

Other differences existed in relative values. Mr Shaw probably paid less for his house than for his clothes. Synge Street was rented at some thirty-odd pounds a year; a gentleman's clothing, according to *The Habits of Good Society* (1855), should not cost more than a tenth of his income, the basic wardrobe comprising four morning coats, a frock-coat, a dress coat and an overcoat (total cost £18); six pairs of morning and one of evening trousers (£9); and four morning waistcoats and an evening waistcoat (£4). Total £31. Mr Shaw may have done without some of these, but on the other hand he also needed hats, gloves, boots and other accessories; so it seems reasonable to conclude that clothes cost him more per annum than the rent. Perhaps things became a little easier for him in the eighteen-sixties, when the modern most-purposes lounge suit began to be regulation daytime wear.

Mrs Shaw's wardrobe must have been at least as expensive. In engravings and early photos the mid-Victorian lady looks a dowdy and unsexy figure, wrapped up in her shawl and bonnet and draped in voluminous materials from neck to feet. Nevertheless, Victorian gentlemen successfully adapted their emotions and thrilled with lust at a glimpse of ankle.

The quantity of clothing on a lady's back was often deplored by moralists, and is surprising in view of the Victorians' dedication to domestic economy. Probably extravagance in quantity was a compensation for the extravagances in colour and cut which were no longer acceptable. Skirts grew wider and wider, bolstered by multiple layers of petticoats that must have roasted the lower limbs. (No wonder the Victorian heroine was said to conceal 'hidden fires'.) Then, in about 1856, a contraption was introduced that maximized skirt-size: the crinoline. This was a rigid wooden structure like a birdcage, over which the skirt was draped. With the help of the crinoline, women now floated along as if in enormous semi-balloons, taking up several places on public transport seats and making small rooms seem even smaller. *Punch* sniggered and moralists fumed — though the crinoline actually made for better-ventilated ladies, since the cage obviated the need for quantities of padding.

Mid-Victorian lady in typical dress

Criticism proved powerless to influence fashion, and the crinoline dominated the 'fifties and early 'sixties. When it was finally discarded, around 1865, little George Bernard Shaw received the shock of his nine-year-old life: the first time his mother appeared without a crinoline he believed she had undergone major surgery, entailing the removal of most of that swollen mass which characterized the adult female anatomy. This change of fashion was the culmination of some gradual changes. The mass of the skirt had shifted to the back, until finally the crinoline skirt gave way to one with a bustle; indoors, the dress was still worn long, with a train that swept the ground — no doubt depreciating fast as it did so, and causing many an economy-minded husband to regret the passing of the crinoline.

Clothing three children — two of them girls — was another of Mr Shaw's expenses. And then there were everyday outgoings on food and drink, entertainments, transport, and so on. This was probably where the economies were made — in the expenditures that people outside the family would never know about. Nobody ever seems to have had a good dinner at the Shaws'; or at any rate nobody (inside or outside the family) ever thought one worth mentioning. The children's staple fare, consumed in the kitchen, was an unpalatable beef and potato stew, washed down by tea that had been equally thoroughly stewed on the hob. And though Mr and Mrs Shaw no doubt did rather better (or at least more ceremoniously) there is no trace of the kind of lavish multi-course spreads to which the Shaws' contemporary, Charles Dickens, devoted so much mouth-watering prose.

Economy was reinforced by Mrs Shaw's distaste for housekeeping. The servants, like the children, were largely left to their own devices, which must have meant barely adequate meals at best. It was probably not even economical, since ill-paid and badly supervised servants are hardly likely to avoid waste or resist a little pilfering. But however bad the food, nobody went hungry. George Carr Shaw insisted on that as he insisted on few things. As one of the widowed Frances Shaw's eleven children he knew what it was to have an empty belly; and he decreed that there should always be abundant bread and butter on the kitchen table, available to the children at any time of the day.

The Shaws seem to have gone out little and entertained even less, though they occasionally visited Bushy Park for family meetings and musical evenings. To get there — and most other places, including the office — a gentleman needed to own a carriage or take a cab. Only a six-hundred-a-year man could contemplate owning a carriage; so Shaw took cabs. But even this was not cheap — especially when gentlemanly munificence was taken into account. *Noblesse oblige.*

	s.	d.
To Driver	1	6
To small boy, seated at driver's feet, whipping the horse, and exciting him with cries of '*Yup*'	0	6
To man, for holding on our luggage, by embracing it with extended arms	1	0
	2	6

This was actually paid by two rather flippant Oxford undergraduates who were just starting a tour of Ireland — and who were evidently unable to add up. But it does give quite a good idea of relative values (including their willingness to employ a living 'holder' rather than bother with a rope). The undergraduates' two and sixpence, or three shillings — the cost of a short journey from the station to their hotel — represented an eighth of one of Mr Shaw's three hundred pounds, or almost a week's wages for his housemaid.

All this talk of money and prices is particularly appropriate to a household like the Shaws'. The upper classes are often above worrying about money, and the poor below or beyond it. The middle class worries. Frayed cuffs, boots that are decaying for want of the price of timely repair, subscriptions overdue: these are the small tragedies of shabby-genteel life, and the more tragic because they do seem small and cannot be confessed to outsiders. It hardly seems like *real* poverty when compared with the slum-dweller's existence; but the comparison misses the point. Shabby-genteel suffering is not physical but mental — a demoralizing load of shame and furtive anxiety. What matters is that *in his own terms* the shabby-gentleman is poor (just as a present-day Spanish peasant is poor in *his* terms, and would not thank you for telling him that his standard of living is high by comparison with that of most Asians). And the shabbier he becomes, the more he insists upon his gentility.

30

Though money worries darkened the atmosphere at Synge Street, the early years were tolerable enough on the surface. In 1857 Mrs Shaw went to visit her father at Kinlough in Leitrim, taking Lucy with her. George Carr Shaw wrote to her almost every day, filling his letters with the doings of one-year-old Bob, whose nurse was encouraging him to start walking in time for his mother's return. Bob and Yup have both fallen out of bed on to their heads; Bob has a new 'Tuscan' hat costing all of ten shillings; Mr Shaw takes Bob out in the perambulator — still a comparative novelty that had replaced a sort of cart drawn along by the nurse. The writing is fluent and easy, the tone is affectionate, and Shaw hazarded some excruciating puns: when Bob fell over backwards and his head went through a pane of glass, his loving father recorded that the little boy escaped unscathed — without so much as a *pane* in his head. We get an impression of a quiet life, mainly involving regular visits to relations — Mr Shaw's sisters, little Bob's godmother, even his Great-Aunt Ellen Whitcroft (though if the intention was to make her relent financially, the visit was a failure).

Of course the letters only tell us Mr Shaw's point of view; Mrs Shaw's replies have not survived. The tranquillity suggested by the letters may actually have existed, for Mrs Shaw had three small children to cope with, and is known to have given them more attention in these early years — when they had something of the charm and helplessness of small animals — than she ever did afterwards. In other words she had something to occupy her, so that life was at least bearable. It can hardly have been more, given the Shaws' temperaments and habits. Bessie was what is often called 'cold', meaning that she disliked being touched and rarely formed passionate attachments. The type is common in life, but tends to be overlooked because most of our notions of character are drawn from fiction, which exalts intense relationships. As a cliché, 'cold' goes with 'haughty' and often with 'domineering', 'cruel', etc. In reality, people like Mrs Shaw are often gay, spirited and altruistic: they are simply not 'personal', and usually seek fulfilment in a vocation rather than in family life. That being so, Mrs Shaw was another square peg in a round hole.

For a fastidious woman, George Carr Shaw was hard to put up with. He drank too much, though he was not an alcoholic or, strictly speaking, a drunkard. (Mrs Shaw's honeymoon story smacks of wild exaggeration. How could the bridegroom empty enough bottles to fill a wardrobe without ever smelling, slurring or staggering? The fact that Mrs Shaw noticed nothing before opening the wardrobe suggests that it contained no more than a couple of beer bottles.) Most evenings Mr Shaw was not drunk, but he was definitely not sober either. He never drank at home or went out with cronies, but nipped out again and again for a quick one at a nearby grocer-publican's. He was fuddled but, fortunately, rather withdrawn and not the least bit violent; the worst he ever did was to smash an ornament on the floor in a rare fit of irritation. So he was not impossible at home in Synge Street. On convivial occasions he was poor company since he was a miserable drunk, full of remorse for his failure to live up to teetotal principles. This anti-social trait was a far more serious offence than heavy drinking, which was hardly unknown in Dublin; and the Shaws were less welcome guests at Bushy Park because of it.

Mrs Shaw may or may not have minded a degree of social isolation, but her attitude to drinking was never in doubt — and was transmitted to the children. As a small boy, Sonny — as 'Bob' had now been rechristened — went for a walk with Mr Shaw by the canal. In hilarious mood Mr Shaw pretended to throw him in — counterfeiting with such vigour that he came close to success. Back home, Sonny told Mrs Shaw of his incredible suspicion that Mr Shaw was drunk.

'When is he ever anything else?' answered Mrs Shaw.

Hemmed in by drink, penury and ever-larger, ever-noisier children, Mrs Shaw lived in a state of mounting frustration. Then a saviour appeared, not astride a white charger but . . . limping elegantly.

Lee and the Life of Music

One of George John Lee's legs was shorter than the other, yet he moved about easily without the aid of a stick. He was one of those men who have the gift of making things look easy, with a dominating personality, a ready flow of speech and boundless energy. His complexion was gypsy-dark and his hair was a glossy black, worn long in 'artistic' fashion. He dressed with fastidious elegance, and in the 'sixties shaved his lip and chin but sported dundrearies — long side whiskers which had become the height of London fashion after the appearance of a fictional character called Lord Dundreary in Tom Taylor's comedy *Our American Cousin.*

Altogether Lee had the equipment of a ladykiller and charlatan; and there may have been elements of both in his character. But he was much more than a mere spellbinder. He was a man with a mission. He was the apostle of music — self-appointed — to the people of Dublin.

Lee's training for the role was sketchy, to say the least. His father had died when Lee was twelve, and he and his brother had been brought up by Mrs Lee; so he presumably had to earn his own living at an early age. There is no record of Lee at any academy of music. When he was eighteen or nineteen he took some lessons from two of Dublin's leading musicians; and when next heard of, at twenty-two, he was already earning his living by teaching singing, and acting as an accompanist on the piano.

He was also the conductor and moving force of the Amateur Music Society, an organization then (1852) as obscure as its name suggests. This was to be the main vehicle of Lee's ambition, and he energetically sought out new recruits; if he passed a house in which an instrument was being competently played, he would knock on the door and persuade the player to join the Society's orchestra. Like a sensible man he pushed on with such instrumentalists as he could muster, giving them the stimulus of actual performance even if the ensemble lacked some of the instruments specified by the composer. And no doubt he was already surrounded by admirers and disciples.

By 1853 Lee was doing well enough to move into a house in Harrington Street with his mother and brother. The new house was just round the corner from the Shaws' place in Synge Street, which was not in the same class. A few years later, Lee was able to take a holiday in Italy. On his way back he saw the well-known tenor Badiali perform in London. Badiali's technique, which gave him a fine voice that lasted into old age, agreed with some of Lee's developing ideas, and the Dublin teacher went on to elaborate a complete system of teaching singing which his disciples soon referred to with reverence as 'The Method'. It required continued application by the pupil over a period of four years. Lee was no threat to teachers who promised to turn their charges into opera stars after twelve lessons, though his rigour may well have discomfited them; only a man of his personal magnetism was likely to have stayed in business without making similar concessions. As he also dismissed the current teaching jargon as verbiage (with much justice), Lee was far from popular with other music teachers — whom, for that matter, he was in the habit of lumping together as quacks.

When Mrs Shaw decided to take some singing lessons, she unwittingly took a step that was to change her whole life. Quite when she did so is unclear. It could have been any time from 1853, when the Lees moved into Harrington Street; but though Mrs Shaw must often have seen the limping maestro on the street, she probably began to take lessons from him some time in the early 'sixties, when the children were starting to be less of a nuisance. Had it happened before 1859 the Method would not have existed and Lee would not have been able to teach it to Mrs Shaw — which he certainly did. And it seems significant that in the early 'sixties Lee's fortunes took a marked turn for the better.

For Mrs Shaw became the most useful as well as the most fanatical of Lee's followers. In music, Lee and the Method she at last found a cause and a reason for living. In time the Method gave her a splendid mezzo-soprano voice and made her the star performer of the Amateur Music Society. Lee found her assistance invaluable, and she was soon his right-hand woman, helping with the organization of con-

Mrs Shaw's singing lesson with Lee

certs, lending a hand at rehearsals, and performing a variety of tasks on which she could bring to bear the formal training in which Lee seems to have been deficient. She was his copyist and arranger, often boldly using the piano score as the basis for a full orchestral version of her own devising. Once dedicated to music, she even set some popular contemporary verses and had them published under the pseudonym 'Hilda'. It must be confessed that titles like 'The Night is Closing Round, Mother', 'Silver Music Ringing' and 'The Parting Hour' do not encourage research into her efforts, let alone revivals.

In the 'sixties the Amateur Music Society began to flourish mightily. From musical evenings, helped out by regimental bands, it progressed to seasons of Grand Concerts held in the Antient Concert Rooms in Great Brunswick Street. The Society began to advertise in *Saunders' News-Letter* and to be reviewed in the *Freeman's Journal* and the *Irish Times,* which commented favourably on the distinction of the singers, the excellence of Lee's conducting and the fashionable nature of the audience, which on occasion included the Lord-Lieutenant and his suite. By 1866 the Amateur Music Society had become 'this favourite society' and Mrs Shaw was 'so well known in musical circles as a gifted amateur vocalist'. Since provincial newspapers generally praise local amateurs, some of the enthusiasm must be taken with a pinch of salt, but all the same the Press record of the 'sixties and 'seventies is impressive in its unanimity. The culmination of this earlier period was probably a vigorously advertised 'Musical and Literary Entertainment', held by the Society at the Antient Concert Rooms to celebrate the tercentenary of Shakespeare's birth. The entertainment took place on the traditional day, 23rd April. Reserved tickets, on sale at Pigott's Musical Warehouse in Grafton Street, cost four shillings; unreserved seats were only two and sixpence. (Such occasions were evidently not for housemaids.) The programme began in best Victorian fashion with a recitation: S. N. Elrington Esq.'s *Ode to Shakespeare,* delivered by a Professor Bell. There was also a prologue written and read 'by William Scribble, Esq.' which sounds like some semi-private joke. The band of the 86th Regiment performed selections from Verdi's *Otello*, while the Society's instrumentalists rendered Mendelssohn's *Midsummer Night's Dream* and selections from Purcell's *Tempest* and Locke's *Macbeth*. The singers performed miscellaneous Shakespeare settings in the

36

shape of choruses, duets, trios, and even a 'Quartette' ('Under the Greenwood Tree'). For an amateur society this was an impressively varied programme, indicating that the Lee-Shaw partnership was becoming steadily more ambitious.

Mrs Shaw's plunge into a musical career would have caused less surprise in the 1860s than it would today. For one thing, full-time amateurism was acceptable in a lady since it was in any case unthinkable for her to take paid employment. And the serious practice of music was far less unusual in Victorian times than it is now. As everybody knows, the Victorians had to entertain themselves instead of watching television or listening to the radio, tapes or records. One result was that some kind of musical skill was widespread: both ladies and gentlemen played and harmonized at the piano, and many played other instruments too. Between them the Shaws, for example, could muster a small if eccentrically constituted band. Mr Shaw vamped competently on the trombone and had been known to join like-minded brass-fanciers and parade along the river bank on summer evenings; he could also play 'Home Sweet Home' on the penny whistle. Of his brothers and sisters, Barney played the ophicleide, Emily the cello, and Charlotte the harp and tambourine. One of the features of a musical evening at Bushy Park was Barney Shaw standing on the ottoman playing 'Annie Laurie', while the rest of the family listened as attentively as a concert audience. Music, then, was a mainstream activity, and the Lee-Shaw effort to bring music to the people was a reputable, understandable venture with no tinge of cultural patronage to it.

Still, one wonders what Mr Shaw made of it all. Mrs Shaw's trips here and there on musical business, and the invasion of the parlour by assorted strangers come to rehearse at the piano, must have had its impact on her husband's quiet, inebriate life. And once she had given herself up to music Mrs Shaw lost all that remained of her interest in the children and the housekeeping. If Mr Shaw didn't like it, there was not much he could do about it. For Mrs Shaw was not one of those who try to dominate others, and who can at least be resisted; she was one of that much smaller, still more effective minority who simply go their own way without even noticing the existence of opposition. A man like George Carr Shaw, ridden with guilt over

The photograph with Lee

his drinking, humbled by his business failures and too inhibited to subdue Bessie with a broomstick, had no choice but to cling to his wife's triumphal chariot.

There is no sign of hostility in the one photograph, probably dating from the mid-'sixties, that shows them all together. Lee is the hero, seated in the centre with his arms folded. Close to him are two female acolytes, one behind him with her hands on his shoulders and one leaning over with her bosom by his ear. At the back, to the left, stands the Amateur Music Society's principal tenor, Charles Cummins, failing to look a swashbuckler despite his big black beard and wide-brimmed 'bohemian' hat. To the right is George Carr Shaw, white-haired but managing to appear rather handsome and dignified; since he seems considerably taller than Cummins and the ladies, he was presumably standing on a box. On the far left, looking soulfully away from both her companions and the photographer, is Bessie Shaw. Her hair is brushed down flat and sleek with oil, and her dress is rich and full — a tunic in some heavy material with embroidered edging, and a long skirt shining in the studio lights. Her aloofness, by contrast with the ladies hanging round Lee, is somehow characteristic of everything we know about her. The age-gap of sixteen years between husband and wife is apparent. Bessie is an attractive woman in the prime of life; George Carr Shaw, however presentable, is on the threshold of old age.

There may have been indirect benefits that made Mrs Shaw's activities more congenial to her husband. Lee was, in effect, an impresario, and it is likely that some of the proceeds from concerts went into his pocket; if they did not, how could he have afforded the time and energy he lavished on his amateurs? And if they did, it is likely that Mrs Shaw benefited too, relieving the strain on the family finances.

Even more tangible benefits followed. In 1866 the whole Shaw family moved out of Synge Street and went to live with Lee at Torca Cottage, high up on Torca Hill where it looks down on Dalkey and the Bay of Dublin. This lovely spot was only nine miles along the coast from Dublin, which was easily accessible by road or rail. Lee and the Shaws stayed there a whole year, the men presumably commuting every weekday. Perhaps there were too many inconveniences entailed; at any rate, they all moved back to Dublin in the spring of 1867.

Torca Cottage overlooking the Bay of Dublin

But they stayed together. Before Torca Cottage, Lee had lived at No. 1 Hatch Street, where he was one of several tenants. It was much better situated than Synge Street, being about half a mile closer to central Dublin and only a few yards south of St Stephen's Green. Lee and the Shaws now took over the whole house, apparently to everyone's satisfaction. Lee had the fashionable address he needed to impress prospective pupils, and at the same time his woman-of-all-work was near at hand whenever he wanted her. The Shaws had moved up in the world, and if the arrangement looks suspiciously like a *ménage à trois* or Eternal Triangle to us, it evidently provoked little comment at the time. No doubt the Shaws represented themselves as the main occupants of the Hatch Street house, with Lee as a sort of superior lodger, though the fact seems to have been that he paid the lion's share of the rent and rates.

The Shaws did lose caste, in spite of their better address; but not because of the household arrangements. And though Mr Shaw's combination of drink and misery was not such as to make his company much sought-after, that too was not the cause of the Shaws' ostracism — though it may have made it seem less regrettable. Their sin was a much more fundamental one: they associated on equal terms with Catholics and tradesmen. Most of Lee's best singers were Catholics. Charles Cummins was a devout Catholic, though at least he was an accountant; but most of the others had not even that saving grace. Lee himself may have been a Catholic in origin (his actual opinions inclined to complete scepticism), though his brother's name — William Harcourt *Nassau* Lee — suggests otherwise. (Nassau is one of the family names of the Orange dynasty in the Netherlands; and William of Orange, as King William III of England, became a Protestant hero by defeating the Catholic forces at the Battle of the Boyne in 1690.) Worst of all, Mrs Shaw's passion for music took her into the Catholic 'chapels' of Dublin; in order to sing Mozart's masses she had to overcome the prejudices instilled by her upbringing, take part in superstitious rites, and hobnob with priests who served the Scarlet Woman.

That was how the matter was seen by George Carr Shaw's cousins. The strength of their purely religious antagonism should not be underestimated: the stark, uncompromising view of the Church of Rome as the Scarlet Woman or Great Whore of Babylon (that is, as an equivalent to the great sinful cities denounced in the Bible) is still to be found in Northern Ireland. Among the 'Anglo-Irish' it was immeasurably strengthened by social snobbery. 'That a son of mine should go to mass with the cook!' wailed one convert's mother; and that sums up the attitude of the Shaw clan. There were no more visits to Bushy Park, and Sonny Shaw later remarked that the children would have been astonished if their parents had gone out of an evening to a dinner or party. Mr Shaw, who was at heart a conventional man (and in any case guiltless of Mozart and masses), may not have relished this social isolation. For Bessie Shaw, the small change of polite social life must now have seemed tedious and trivial. What did such things matter when she had Lee and the life of music?

Growing Up

According to Sonny Shaw, he was about six when his mother 'abandoned' him; her only positive contribution to his education, so far as he remembered, was to teach him half-a-dozen nursery rhymes. There was no unkindness in Mrs Shaw's action: it was simply that the children were becoming less endearing (as children tend to do when they leave toddlerhood) and she was becoming absorbed in musical matters. Besides, her own childhood in Palmerston Place, rigorously supervised by Aunt Ellen Whitcroft, had given Mrs Shaw a horror of discipline in any form; and this genuine feeling served to excuse her neglect of her own children as a granting of freedom. The reality was that Mrs Shaw almost never took them out anywhere, even for a walk; and that they regretted her absence.

Mr Shaw seems to have done his best, between drinks. He went out for walks with Sonny, or took him out to Clibborn & Shaw's mill at the country end of Dolphin's Barn; the boy evidently enjoyed playing round the spot so much that he put up with the long walk. Before Lee came on the scene, Mr Shaw had some semblance of authority and saw to it that the conventions were observed. The children were baptized by the Reverend William Carroll (the brother-in-law who had married Mr and Mrs Shaw), they regularly attended church and Sunday School, and Mr Shaw even led family prayers at home.

But at best Mr Shaw was an uninspiring father. One day, when he found Sonny copying him by pretending to smoke a pipe, he told the boy that he should not take him as a model in anything whatsoever — or only as a model of everything a man should *not* be or do. The lesson was driven home by the discovery of Mr Shaw's drinking habits. The sight of their amiable father, with a joint under one arm and a goose under the other, butting at a wall and making a concertina of his tall hat in the belief that he was pushing open a gate, sent the children into fits of laughter — which concealed their embarrassment and shame. Paradoxically, the most conventional member of the Shaw family circle was also the least worthy of ordinary respect — a fact that must have enormously influenced the development of the Shaw children.

However, for some years the adults closest to the children were the servants. Lucy, Sonny and Aggie were not supposed to associate with children whose parents were 'in trade'; but they were raised by illiterate 'papists' from the slums. The absurdity is not as great as it seems: servants, however undesirable as influences, were too far below the Shaws to threaten them socially; whereas the difference between a Protestant-merchant-gentleman and a Catholic-shop-keeper-'person' was small enough to be eroded by any relaxation of exclusiveness. The easy relations between nobles and peasants — often quoted to the disadvantage of the middle class — is another example of the same phenomenon: absence of rivalry allows a kind of familiarity or even a rough equality.

For much of the time the presence of the children in and out of the kitchen must have been a nuisance. They held up work and interrupted conversation — though in the atmosphere of the Shaw household it was probably not censored for their benefit. Certainly one girl, who was charged with taking Sonny for walks, carried him along to visit her friends in the slum tenements of Dublin; when she met up with gentlemen friends, he even went with her into public houses, though he was too impressed by his father's sober theory or drunken practice to enjoy the soft drinks he was bought. Most of the servants were similarly callous or careless (what else could the Shaws expect for their eight pounds a year?); but, as always, there were exceptions. One, Nurse Williams, tried to safeguard Sonny's soul, as well as looking after his body, by solemnly sprinkling holy water over the poor lost little heretic. The benefits of this practice were evidently limited, since Sonny continued to insist on saying his prayers in bed, though admonished that *warm* prayers could not be pleasing to God.

George Carr Shaw gave his son an important early lesson. He noticed Sonny playing with another boy in the street and questioned him closely about this new friend. To his horror, Sonny told him that the boy's father was an ironmonger. Mr Shaw then explained, in

Governess Miss Hill's lesson

the most impressive terms he could muster, that association with tradespeople was ignoble and dishonouring. The fact that the ironmonger was very prosperous indeed — was irrelevant. The friendship must end at once.

Which it did. Sonny took his father's teaching to heart and became an unmitigated snob; he even tried to drive a little girl — a neighbour — out of his group of playmates, until he was put in his place by an older boy. There was evidently more camaraderie in the street, and probably few parents took class-consciousness quite as far as George Carr Shaw. Still, Mrs Shaw seems to have shared his general attitude during these early years, though she always laughed at the inflated dynastic pride of the Shaw family. The Amateur Music Society was to teach her that musical talent is no respecter of classes and sects, and in time the children were to learn the same lesson.

The children's formal teaching was mainly the work of the governess. Miss Hill taught them to read and write and do sums, though Sonny failed to master division because he couldn't understand what the governess meant by 'into'; presumably, like many children, he never let her know exactly what it was that baffled him. (When he went to school he learned division — and always later swore that it was the only thing he did learn there.) Miss Hill's attempts to inculcate a taste for poetry were less successful: the Shaw children rolled about with mirth when confronted with 'Stop; for thy tread is on an empire's dust'. Which says a good deal for their taste.

Little is known of the girls' childhood. Lucy seems to have been a bold, confident, carefree girl who made friends easily and overshadowed the quieter Agnes and shyer Sonny. Presumably both girls stayed at home, studying under a governess and amusing themselves as best they could; in her teens Lucy developed a promising voice (along with a talent for sight-reading that her mother envied), and began to take part in the Lee-Shaw ventures. Being the boy, Sonny was destined for more academic pursuits. The Reverend William Carroll gave him a good start in Latin; then, when he was almost eleven, Sonny became a day boy at the Wesleyan Connexional School, on the south side of St Stephen's Green. (He seems to have attended the school for a few weeks two years before; why he left is not known.) As the name indicates, the school was a Methodist foundation; but there was nothing in the least strange about a Shaw

— nominally a member of the Church of Ireland — joining it as a pupil. This was one of the peculiar features of Irish life. The equivalent situation in England — a member of the Church of England attending a Dissenting academy — would have been unthinkable; and over thirty years later there were English Nonconformists prepared to go to gaol rather than contribute to the upkeep of Anglican schools. But in Ireland the only distinction that mattered was between Catholic and Protestant. Compared with this, the differences between the Church of Ireland, the Methodists, the Presbyterians and other Protestant sects were regarded as merely technical. If the best school was a Methodist one, parents of other Protestant denominations would gladly send their sons to it.

Wesleyan Connexional was a school of some pretensions, aiming to prepare boys for a scholarly career. It took in boarders as well as day boys (the two groups mutually abusive, as ever), and the curriculum was dominated by the study of Latin, as at the best English schools. Greek was also taught, but Sonny never got that far. However shy he may have been at home, among other boys at school he was deviser of adventurous games in the playground and a chatterbox in class. He learned nothing. The chanting of declensions and conjugations, and the ritual answering of questions by turns, failed to hold his attention, and he was usually bottom of the class. When the Reverend William Carroll examined him in Latin, he discovered that, so far from having progressed, Sonny had forgotten much of his pre-school learning. Wesleyan had failed, and Sonny was taken away from it after little more than a year of irregular attendance.

The following summer — 1867 — was spent at Torca Cottage, which Lee and the Shaws still used for their annual holidays. While they were there, Sonny went to a nearby private school; but when they returned to Hatch Street, the problem of his future had to be faced. At this point Lee took a hand. He had met a teacher at the Central Model Boys' School in Marlborough Street, had been impressed by what he heard, and suggested to the Shaws that Sonny should try it. Sonny did; and Sonny hated it. The Central Model was multi-denominational but in fact predominantly Catholic — and distinctly lower middle class in ethos. Though the Shaws themselves were *declassé* — or perhaps because they were — Sonny clung to his father's prejudices. Indeed they became so deeply ingrained that he never quite got over the shame of going to Marlborough Street; and only 'confessed' when he was in his eighties — after a lifetime's work as an egalitarian socialist with no conventional religious creed! Not surprisingly, after only a few months at the school Sonny rebelled; backed by Mr Shaw, he simply refused to go any more.

This was a pity, since the Central Model seems to have been a good school by Dublin standards — certainly better than the Wesleyan, which, with all its pretensions, was not much more than an over-crowded, insanitary house in which boys were kept from under their parents' feet at a cost of six or seven guineas a year. At the Central Model, Sonny steadied down and did rather better in class; and during breaks he spent most of his time with the masters, who were favourably impressed by his knowledge of the arts.

For, despite his aversion to school, Sonny was clever and sensitive; and there was plenty to nourish his intelligence at home. Like many another self-taught genius, he read without stint — *The Arabian Nights, Pilgrim's Progress,* Shakespeare, Dickens: none of them yet school classics, and so not yet impossible of enjoyment. And as the Shaw household was always filled with music, Sonny and his sisters had an unparalleled education in this respect. Though not as gifted as Lucy, Sonny soon developed a highly discriminating ear, learned to hum every note of *Don Giovanni* and other masterworks, and incidentally picked up a large number of French and Italian phrases that could be effectively flourished in conversation.

Adult society at Hatch Street was an education in itself, though of a peculiar sort. Absorption in music and a general carelessness of social forms did not create an atmosphere favourable to the development of little ladies and gentlemen. The young Shaws failed to learn the niceties of Victorian social drill at an age when it should have been becoming second nature, and took years to acquire the kind of confidence it gave; though they had plenty of the careless Bohemian high-spirits and self-assertion that never quite came off in good society — especially when the Bohemian had less money than everybody else present.

On the other hand, everyone talked freely at Hatch Street, and the children listened to discussions which would not have been allowed at all in most establishments. They were given added spice by the frequent presence of Bessie Shaw's brother, Walter Gurly, who had

48

taken a job as ship's doctor with the Inman Line, and stayed at Hatch Street between voyages. Gurly fascinated Sonny with his combination of wit, intelligence, blasphemy and blue language; and in conversation he was the perfect complement to the conventional Mr Shaw and the forceful, earnest Lee. One story which gets the likeness of all three, concerns a discussion of the raising of Lazarus. Mr Shaw accepted the Biblical account; Lee rejected it as a scientific impossibility; and Uncle Walter maintained that it was a put-up job between Lazarus and Jesus.

No wonder Sonny had set up as the Aesthete and Boy Atheist by the time he entered his teens. His father's snobbery aside, Lee was probably the strongest influence on his development — not because there was any special liking between them, but because Sonny recognized in Lee a man of real personal force who was prepared to ignore received opinion and think for himself about any subject under the sun; that, in fact, is more than anything else what Sonny learned from Lee. But he also took over a number of Lee's cranky, thoroughly sensible habits — eating brown bread instead of white, for example (which in those days seemed like wilful barbarism), sleeping with a window open, and distrusting the medical profession. From Mr Shaw, Sonny took a snobbery of which he was already ashamed (though the feeling could coexist with a kind of shame that was purely snobbish) and a devastating, hilarious penchant for anti-climax; in Mr Shaw this had the effect of destroying his occasional efforts to voice serious opinions — as when he solemnly told Sonny that it was wrong to sneer at a great book like the Bible, of which its worst enemy could say no more than that it was the damndest parcel of lies ever written. Since Mr Shaw really believed the contrary, it is clear that this habit of self-deflation represented a defeated man's way of anticipating his defeat; but it was not the ideal method of guiding or instructing the young.

Mrs Shaw gave no guidance at all. She was a remote, glamorous figure whom Sonny worshipped but could never get close to; and the more remote for being not the least unkind, never hitting the children or becoming involved with them by losing her temper. Sonny always admired his mother's character and to some extent modelled himself on her. (In later life he was to put art and civic improvement above lighthearted, spare-time activities such as personal relations.) At the same time he never really forgave Bessie Shaw. Her neglect, his father's drinking, and social shame combined to make his childhood a torment that he always referred to — even as an old man — with utter repulsion.

Meanwhile, there was yet another school, this time rather nearer home, in Aungier Street, only a minute's walk from St Peter's Church. The English, Scientific and Commercial Day School was lodged in a Georgian mansion that sounds rather too good for it — the sometime town house of Lord Aungier, containing broad staircases and spacious rooms with stuccoed ceilings and fine oak mantelpieces. The school was thoroughly Protestant but set its sights lower than the Wesleyan: instead of preparing young gentlemen for a university, it prepared young men for business — which in real terms meant that there was no attempt to teach Latin, and that some sort of attention was given to the composition of English and the mathematics of money.

Sonny was reasonably happy at his new school, though it cannot be said that he left with a high opinion of this or any other educational establishment. He now made some efforts in class and became one of the leading pupils. However, he remained rebellious enough to stand up for Ireland against the textbooks' preoccupation with England and England's affairs. In this too he may have been influenced by Lee, who was strongly in favour of Home Rule. These were the years of Fenian conspiracy and Gladstone's great Irish reforms; but outside Sonny's school essays they seem to have had no impact on the world of the Shaws.

At Aungier Street the best boy at prose composition had been Matthew Edward McNulty, who now had to divide honours with Sonny Shaw; and in spite of the rivalry these two became close friends. (A significant contrast to Sonny's behaviour at the Central Model, where only the teachers were good enough for him.) Together they read an early boys' magazine called *Boys of England,* ran a short-lived school drama club which Sonny undermined by guying the heroes and heroines of Shakespearian tragedy, and got into scrapes of the orthodox window-breaking type. But their great passion was drawing, in which they took extra lessons at four shillings a quarter, though they seem to have benefited more from regular visits

George Bernard Shaw as a junior clerk

to the excellent collection at the National Gallery. Sonny dreamed of becoming another Michelangelo, though on occasion he rejected this in favour of founding a new world religion. McNulty already knew that he wanted to be a writer, and probably stimulated Sonny's earlier efforts. The most noteworthy of these was *Strawberrinos: or, the Haunted Winebin,* apparently a verse entertainment on the lines of Gilbert and Sullivan operettas — fun, of course, but significantly preoccupied with drunkenness.

Soon it was time to leave school and get a job. At about fourteen Sonny applied for a position with a firm of cloth merchants — apparently on his own initiative, since he allowed one of the partners to persuade him that he should stay at school for another year. Then, in November 1871, when he was just over fifteen years old, Sonny was taken on as junior clerk by a firm of land agents, C. Uniacke Townshend & Co. of Molesworth Street. A land agent was pretty much what we should call an estate agent, though collection of rents and estate management made up a larger part of the business than it does in most modern firms. It also ranked as a profession in Ireland, and was therefore an acceptable occupation for a Shaw. Sonny got the job through the influence of Mr Shaw's brother in the Irish Valuation Office, whose position made him a man that any land agent was pleased to oblige. The conditions show the value put upon gentility. Sonny was paid eighteen shillings a month — a specially low salary, since he had not paid a premium to enter the office and so ranked below the university-educated 'gentlemen apprentices' who had; and whereas each gentleman apprentice was addressed as 'Mr', Sonny was plain 'Shaw'. The fact that George Carr Shaw could do no better than this for his only son — could not put up a premium or afford to take Sonny on at Clibborn & Shaw — confirms that the family was still painfully hard-up.

As it happened, Sonny did surprisingly well. For the first year or so he was no more than the office boy, fetching and carrying and sticking on stamps; his most responsible job was to copy and file letters and documents — copying being one of the chief clerical tasks in the age before speed-typing and the photo-copy machine. Then, in February 1873, the firm's cashier absconded with as much of the takings as he could lay his hands on; young Shaw was given the job until a replacement could be found; and he did it so well that the

Sonny and McNulty

idea of a replacement was soon forgotten. As cashier he had to handle large sums of money, collecting and paying over debts, insurances and rents, keeping careful accounts, taking and giving receipts, and generally combining business aplomb with clerical accuracy. When he travelled on business, he went first class, expenses paid. His salary quickly rose to £48 a year, and by the time he was twenty had reached the strikingly high figure of £84. (Compare this with the London clerk in John Davidson's poem, supporting a wife and children on 'thirty bob a week' at the end of the century.) Even supposing that he made generous contributions to the family budget, Sonny Shaw must have been a prosperous young bachelor. He was certainly able to brave the ridicule of family and friends in a new morning coat and silk hat, to buy season tickets for musical and artistic events, and to pay a visit to his bosom friend McNulty, who was working at a branch of the Bank of Ireland in Newry.

While Shaw was there the friends were photographed together; and it comes as a shock to realize how young they were — only eighteen, and by today's standards an immature-looking eighteen despite the bulky formal jackets and waistcoats. And, in fact, these two sober men of business were also romantic adolescents who wrote each other long letters, swore blood-brotherhood and utter frankness, and dreamed of literary fame while getting bogged down in a projected *Newry Nights' Entertainment* which would presumably have been a little less exotic than its Arabian prototype. Even in the office Shaw sometimes got into trouble for leading the apprentices in operatic choruses; but on the whole business and romance occupied separate compartments of his being. Which did not prevent him from heartily detesting his promising career and longing for some compelling reason to abandon it.

Meanwhile, however, the activities of the older generation had moved to a sudden crisis.

Triumphs and Departures

From the end of the eighteen-sixties Lee had one success after another. His concerts featured the best-loved vocal music of the day, by Verdi, Rossini, Mozart, Gounod, Mendelssohn, Handel, Meyerbeer and Donizetti, giving his singers a training in preparation for still more ambitious projects. In 1869 Lee himself launched into authorship with *The Voice: Its Artistic Production, Development and Preservation,* which did well enough to warrant a second edition the following year, this time with simultaneous publication in London. Lee may have had some help with the parts of the book dealing with anatomy, and perhaps with the style — his own being rather clogged, to judge by his surviving letters. *The Voice* was a thoroughly competent exposition, most of which could stand unchanged today. But Lee gave away no professional secrets: the would-be singer was advised to — take lessons.

From 1871 the Amateur Musical Society gave some of its concerts in the chief Dublin theatres, the Theatre Royal and the Gaiety; Lee's ambitions were growing with every year. Another sign of this was a change of name: from December 1871 he became G. V. Lee, which soon bloomed into G. Vandeleur Lee. He may well have been adopting the name of the man he believed to be his real father, a Colonel Vandeleur of Kilrush, County Clare, where Lee was born; but whatever the reason, the change suggests the presence of incipient megalomania.

For Lee and Mrs Shaw, 1872-3 was the climax of their Dublin careers. To exploit the International Exhibition of 1872, Lee transformed the Amateur Musical Society into the grandiosely-named New Philharmonic, and organized a series of concerts at the Exhibition Palace. The choirs, led by Mrs Shaw, regularly numbered four or five hundred performers — an impressive figure by almost any standards. The Dublin Musical Festival, held at the beginning of 1873, marked the high point of Lee's whole career. The festival seems to have been entirely his affair; involved the importation of the famous singers Tietjens and Agnesi; was patronized by the Lord-Lieutenant and his lady; and induced the Dublin Tramways Co. to run late cars. The choice of Handel's *Messiah* was doubly appropriate, since the oratorio had received its very first performance in Dublin, and also because it suggested comparisons with the Three Choirs Festivals which had been held in English cathedral towns since the eighteenth century. There could be no greater musical distinction than this — in the provinces; and Lee may now have begun to think about trying his luck in London.

At any rate, towards the end of the 1873-4 season he organized a joint benefit performance for himself and his friend Michael Levey, leader of the Theatre Royal orchestra. Then a few days later Mrs Shaw scored a triumph as the gypsy Azucena in Verdi's *Il Trovatore*, again at the Theatre Royal. The Dublin *Evening Mail* praised the young lady (who was forty-four at the time) but suggested she should make-up more thoroughly in order to look older — intentionally or not, a charming compliment.

Then came the earthquake. In May, after Lee's next concert, he quarrelled violently with the composer Sir Robert Stewart, and by the first week of June — seemingly as a result — had left Dublin for good. Nobody knows exactly what the quarrel was about, but Stewart undoubtedly believed he had shown up Lee as an 'imposter' and driven him from Ireland. Stewart probably resented the evolution of the Amateur Musical Society into a performing body that challenged professional musicians and threatened their livelihood; and it may have been Lee's pretensions in this area that he attacked. Lee was hardly an imposter or charlatan in any other sense, since his abilities as a singing teacher and impresario and conductor of amateurs are unchallengeable. Stewart's point of view would have been influenced by his own lust for power: the defeat of Lee enabled him to take over the New Philharmonic and become musical dictator of Dublin. Did Lee leave because Stewart 'exposed' him? Or because Stewart's hostility would have made his further progress impossible? Or simply because Dublin had no more to offer his ambition? It is not likely we shall ever know.

Lee's departure had an immediate and drastic effect on the Shaws.

Within a fortnight Mrs Shaw had followed his example, taking Agnes with her — an action which, inevitably, brings into question the exact nature of her relationship with Lee. In later years Sonny Shaw always asserted that Mrs Shaw left out of financial necessity, the withdrawal of Lee's contribution having unbalanced the family budget. But this is an unlikely story on several counts. The family could not have been doing so very badly, since Sonny as well as Mr Shaw was bringing in money; London has never been the place one goes to in order to retrench; and Mrs Shaw was more likely to have succeeded in her intended profession as a singing teacher in Dublin, where she was known, than in the vastness and anonymity of London.

Given the coincidence of dates, the conclusion is inescapable: that Mrs Shaw left Dublin because life without Lee was insupportable. That he was therefore also her lover, or even the father of her children (as some writers have suggested), are speculations of no great interest since there is no evidence one way or the other — except the entire absence of gossip about them, which in Dublin presupposed inhuman discretion on somebody's part. (They did not, of course, live together in London: without the presence of Mr Shaw that would have meant instant social ruin.) Besides, if there was a liaison, it cannot have been burning with a hard, gem-like flame after so many years; so whatever their physical relations, if Bessie Shaw followed Lee it must have been because he was the source of everything exciting and meaningful in her life — teaching, practising, rehearsing, arranging, organizing, performing. From this point of view Dublin must have been far less attractive for Lee's followers under Stewart's régime, and it is worth noting that Lee's other two stars, Charles Cummins and his wife Annie, dropped right out of the city's musical life after his departure.

Mrs Shaw's decision caused amazingly little fuss within the family. Perhaps the Shaws recognized their incompatibility and were glad to part now that the children had more or less grown up. Or perhaps the break was not immediately recognized as such. Aggie's health (she was tubercular) may have provided a sufficient excuse for the journey to England. As ever, then, there was no unkindness. 'The Par' and 'the Mar' exchanged letters; Mr Shaw sent Lucy a pair of boots shortly after she too joined Mrs Shaw in search of musical

57

fame; and when George Carr Shaw and Sonny moved out of Hatch Street, Mrs Shaw came back to Dublin and supervised the operation. There was, however, an irony in the situation: the husband that Mrs Shaw left was a rigid teetotaller; his conversion had been effected by fright about two years before, after he had collapsed in a mild fit on the doorstep.

The reformed Mr Shaw was a tolerable room-mate for Sonny in their lodgings at 61 Harcourt Street; and Sonny stuck it out for another two years. Deprived of music, he belatedly taught himself to pick out tunes on the piano and tried to develop his voice; wrote bulky letters to McNulty; and dreamed of conquering London. The final push was his replacement as cashier by C. Uniacke Townshend's nephew. Though Shaw's salary was not cut, he resented the demotion and probably realized for the first time that family and money were more important than hard work in the narrow world of Dublin; without money and more substantial family influence than he could muster, he would never amount to more than a clerk — chief clerk, head cashier, trusted and respected perhaps, but still a clerk. And that would never do. On 29th February 1876 he gave the firm a month's notice, stating that he objected to receiving a salary which he did not earn — a broad hint at the nature of his grievance. Townshend was sorry to lose him, and perhaps unwilling to antagonize Valuation Office Shaw; so he offered to reinstate him. This must have been a sore temptation, but Sonny stuck to his guns, having determined to be 'a professional man of genius'. His intentions towards the world of work are revealed by the fact that he either refused a testimonial or threw it away; three years later, when Mr Shaw obtained one from Townshend's and sent it to a prospective employer, his son was furious — especially since it got him the job despite his efforts to represent himself as unemployable. But for the moment he was about to become a free man. Friday 31st March was his last day in the office — four days after Agnes had died in a nursing home at Ventnor on the Isle of Wight. A few days later Sonny sat for photographs with two friends from the office, packed his carpet bag, and boarded a steamer from one of Dublin's quays, on the North Wall of the Liffey.

And then there was one — Mr Shaw, sole survivor of the Dublin household.

Afterwards

The end of the Dublin household should also be the end of this study. But it seems right to wind up a Victorian story by following the tradition of the Victorian novel and telling the reader what became of the characters after they went their ways.

Mr Shaw spent the rest of his life in lodgings, supported by the small profits of Clibborn & Shaw. When McNulty returned to Dublin he often visited Sonny's father, who spent much of his time reading the financial news in the Chamber of Commerce or poring over his accounts. George Carr Shaw saw his wife only once more, when he visited London for a few days, and the children almost never wrote to him. In his last years he developed a few mild eccentricities. He died, aged seventy-one, in 1885. His profession is recorded as 'miller', and he is buried at Mount Jerome Cemetery, the last resting-place of genteel Dublin Protestants.

Lee failed to make an impact on London. He rented a house in Park Lane and gave lessons, but the rigours of the Method had little appeal to metropolitan socialites. Soon he was forced to promise miraculous results after a dozen lessons, like the Dublin teachers he had once denounced. Mrs Shaw, offended by this betrayal of the Method, dropped Lee (it is possible too that she caught him making eyes at Lucy). But in any case he had no chance of promoting anything more ambitious than Gilbert and Sullivan: London was well-endowed musically, and there would be no crowds flocking to amateur grand opera. Still, Lee kept afloat (though sometimes by dubious means) until his death in 1886, aged about fifty-six. Characteristically, none of the Shaws attended his funeral.

Bessie Shaw's first London home was at No. 13 Victoria Grove (now Netherton Grove), a cul-de-sac off the Fulham Road; and it was there that Lucy and Sonny joined her. In the early years Mrs Shaw was closely involved in Lee's Park Lane activities, and took the overflow of his pupils. Later, after some hard times as a private teacher — largely supported by the Gurly money, though Mr Shaw seems to have helped a bit as well — Bessie began to teach choirs in schools. Here her artistic talent and commanding personality brought splendid results — so much so that she was almost eighty before the principal of the North London Collegiate School for girls could be persuaded to let her retire. In her last years she was much interested in spiritualism; even in the eighteen-sixties she had experimented with the planchette, which was then new to Ireland. At various times she contacted Agnes, Lee and her husband, though without any startling communications. Perhaps she had better luck after her death in 1913.

In Dublin, Lucy had sung Amina in Bellini's *La Sonnambula,* one of Lee's last productions. In London she too dropped him after a year or so; their personal relations had never been easy (each brought out the 'temperamental' in the other), and Lucy soon realized that Lee could do nothing for her beyond a part in an amateur performance of *Patience.* She then went on the stage professionally, taking the name Lucy Carr Shaw, and achieved a measure of success in musical comedy. In particular, she toured the provinces with *Dorothy* (now forgotten, but the *Sound of Music* of its day), in which she played the title role. She never made the West End, and her career, begun late, finished prematurely. Like her sister, Lucy was attacked by consumption, and although she survived until 1920, the last two decades of her life were spent as an invalid, supported by her brother.

When McNulty visited the Shaws in London, he met Lucy for the first time — a surprising fact which illustrates the extent to which the Shaws lived separate lives, aloof from one another. McNulty fell in love with Lucy and proposed to her; but she turned him down, on the grounds that she was older than he — which may, as a reason, have been no more than a polite excuse. McNulty, unlike his friend, stayed in Ireland and went on working for the bank. Not all his dreams were unfulfilled: he did write novels, and one of his plays was performed by Dublin's famous Abbey Theatre. But he never became famous, and his life seems to have been a quiet, uneventful one.

Exactly the opposite was true of McNulty's lifelong friend, Sonny Shaw. Nobody now called him Sonny, of course; his mother and

George Bernard Shaw in later life

sister insisted on calling him George (which name he loathed), but he was gradually to establish himself as Bernard Shaw, and at last, to millions, as 'G.B.S.' For some years after leaving Dublin he toiled at writing novels which nobody would publish, while sedulously avoiding work. He also 'ghosted' music criticisms for Lee, who put many a guinea his way; G.B.S. was the one member of the family who stayed in touch with the maestro until Lee's death, at which time he was ghosting a new edition of *The Voice*. Shaw also threw himself into the socialist revival of the 'eighties, becoming a founder-member of the Fabian Society and a notable platform speaker. As a critic of music, and later of the drama, he came to the forefront of English letters in the 'nineties. Finally, when he was almost forty, he turned to writing plays; and it was as a playwright that he achieved world fame in the years before World War One. His life stretched from mid-Victorian to modern times, only ending in 1950, when he was ninety-four; and the splendour of that life, and the curiosity of biographers, have provided the materials for this little family history.

Suggested Reading

Cullen, L. M., *Life in Ireland* (Batsford, 1968).

Dunbar, J., *The Early Victorian Woman* (Harrap, 1953).

Ervine, St. J., *Bernard Shaw: His Life, Work and Friends* (Constable, 1956).

O'Faolain, S., *The Irish* (Penguin, 1969).

Gorham, M., *Ireland From Old Photographs* (Batsford, 1971).

Henderson, A., *George Bernard Shaw: Man of the Century* (Appleton-Century-Crofts, New York, 1956).

Lawrence, D. H. (ed.), *Bernard Shaw: Collected Letters 1874-97* (Max Reinhardt, 1965).

Pearson, H., *Bernard Shaw: His Life and Personality* (Collins, 1961).

Rosset, B. C., *Shaw of Dublin: The Formative Years* (Pennsylvania State University Press, 1964).

Shaw, G. B., autobiographical prefaces to *Immaturity* (1930) and *London Music in 1888-90* (1937); and *Sixteen Self-Sketches* (1949); all published by Constable. The material has also been Collated into an 'Autobiography' by S. Weintraub (Reinhardt, 1970).

Wildeblood, J. & Brinson, P., *The Polite World: A Guide to English Manners and Deportment from the Thirteenth to the Nineteenth Century* (O.U.P., 1965).